DINO

ALPHABET

Words by Robin Feiner

A is for **A**nkylosaurus.
[an-key-low-sawr-us]
Similar to a crocodile or armadillo,
the Ankylosaurus had huge plates
of bone built into its skin to protect
it against attackers. It also used
its long, strong tail as a club!
Now that's some legendary
body armor!

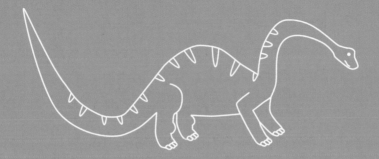

B is for Brontosaurus.
[bron-tah-sawr-us]
With its long neck and even
longer tail, the Brontosaurus was
one of the largest creatures to ever
walk the Earth. By the time it
was 10 years old, it had already
reached full size – about
75 feet tall!

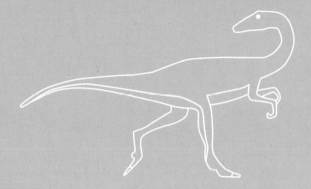

C is for **C**oelophysis.
[seel-oh-fie-sis]
It may have been small,
but this two-legged hunter was
fast! It also had excellent vision
thanks to its big forward-facing
eyes. Coelophysis lived in the
Triassic period, and may have
traveled in packs.

D is for **D**iplodocus.
[di-plo-duh-kuhs]
If you've ever been to a dinosaur museum, chances are you've seen the large skeleton belonging to the Diplodocus on display. This plant-eater with strong legs has also been featured in many popular movies and cartoons.

E is for Einiosaurus.
[eye-knee-o-sawr-us]
With its long snout horn and
neck frills, it's easy to see why
scientists gave it a name meaning
'buffalo lizard!' Einiosaurus was
a plant-eating dinosaur that
most likely lived in herds
with its relatives.

F is for **F**ukuisaurus.
[foo-koo-eye-sawr-us]
Believed to only be about
6 feet tall, the Fukuisaurus was
pretty small for a dinosaur! So far,
scientists have found only one set
of fossil remains (in Japan) of this
rare dinosaur that lived around
129 million years ago.

Gg

G is for Gallimimus.
[gal-ih-my-muss]
This two-legged dinosaur from
the Cretaceous period was fast
and agile – much like an ostrich,
but with a tail! Gallimimus also
had a bird-like beak, which was
shaped like a shovel so it could
easily scoop up food.

H is for **H**ylaeosaurus.
[hi-lay-ah-sawr-us]
One of the first dinosaurs to be discovered, Hylaeosaurus may not have been big, but it was tough – with a big bony plate around its hips, and rows of horns all down its back and shoulders.

I is for Iguanodon.
[ig-wah-na-don]
The Iguanodon had unique
thumbs with spikes on them to
protect it and help it gather food. But
when scientists first discovered this
legendary plant-eater in 1822, they
thought the thumb spike was
its nose!

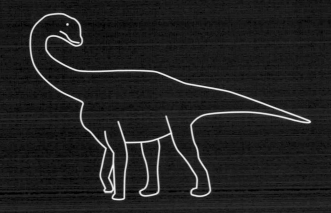

J is for **J**obaria.
[joe-bare-ee-ah]
This West African giant
was one of the most complete
long-necked dinosaur skeletons
ever discovered. Its flexible neck
meant it could stand up on its
back legs to reach food or
fight off attackers.

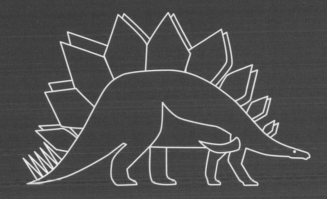

K is for **K**entrosaurus.
[ken-tro-sawr-us]
Originating from the Jurassic
period, this slow-walking dinosaur's
name means 'spiky lizard,' and
that's exactly what it looked like –
with different types of spikes all
the way from its back down
to its tail!

L is for Lambeosaurus.
[lam-bee-o-sawr-us]
Named after Lawrence
Lambe, a Canadian fossil hunter,
Lambeosaurus was the first
duck-billed dinosaur found in
North America. It had a hollow,
bony crest on its head, pebbly
skin and over 1,000 teeth!

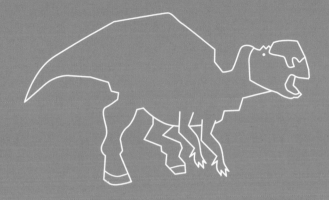

M is for **M**uttaburrasaurus.
[mew-tah-burr-ah-sawr-us]
What sets this Australian
dinosaur apart is its rounded snout
with a bump on the top. Scientists
believe this bump was hollow, which
could have made Muttaburrasaurus'
voice louder and sense of
smell stronger.

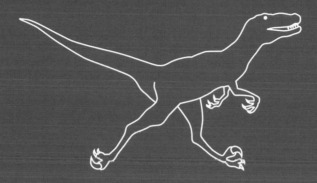

N is for Noasaurus.
[no-ah-sawr-us]
Although it only grew to
be about 3 feet tall and 7 feet
long, this small meat-eater was
still an expert hunter, using its
claws skillfully. Noasaurus lived
in South America, with scientists
finding fossils in northwest
Argentina.

O is for Oviraptor.
[oh-vih-rap-tor]
With its parrot-like head,
three-fingered clawed hands and
powerful jaw, Oviraptor was quite
a unique dinosaur! Found sitting on
a nest, scientists gave it a name
meaning 'egg thief' – but later
discovered it was protecting,
not stealing, the eggs!

P is for **P**terodactyl.
[tare-oh-dack-til]
This creature is often called a
dinosaur but it's actually a type of
'pterosaur,' which is a flying reptile.
With its pointy beak and leathery
wings, the Pterodactyl soared
across the skies during the
Jurassic period.

Q is for Quetzalcoatlus.
[ket-sal-koh-at-lus]
Named after the Aztec
feathered god 'Quetzalcoatl,'
this flying reptile (or pterosaur) used
its large brain and big eyes to spot
its prey from the sky then glided
toward the water and
swooped it up!

R is for **R**ugops.
[roo-gops]
Much about this medium-sized
meat-eater is still a mystery, but
a skull found in the year 2000 led
scientists to believe that the Rugops
may have used special facial features
to make itself seem bigger and
scarier than it actually was!

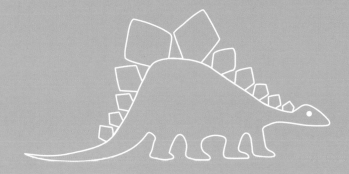

S is for **S**tegosaurus.
[steg-ah-sawr-us]
You probably know what it looks like from a movie or cartoon, but did you know that the Stegosaurus is the State Dinosaur for Colorado? That's because Colorado is where the first Stegosaurus fossil was found!

T is for Tyrannosaurus rex.
[tie-ran-ah-sawr-us-rex]
T. rex was one of the fiercest meat-eaters that ever lived. Around 40 feet long with the most powerful head and biggest teeth of all the dinosaurs, the only creature it had to fear was another T. rex! Legendary!

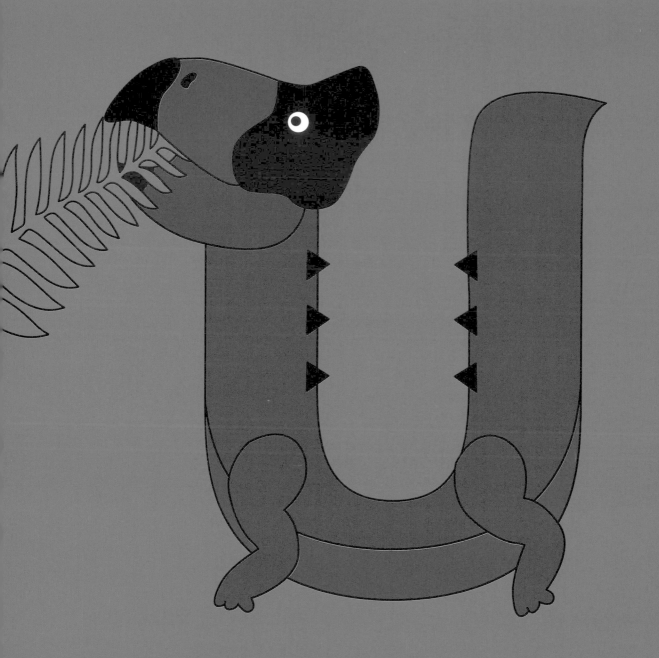

U is for **U**danoceratops.
[u-dan-oh-ser-ah-tops]
First discovered in the Udan-Sayr
area in Mongolia, Udanoceratops
was a horn-faced plant-eater that
used its beak-like mouth to clip off
parts of plants and ferns. It also
had small neck frills and a
solid tail.

V is for **Velociraptor.**
[vell-oss-ee-rap-tor]
If you've ever watched 'Jurassic Park,' you would've seen that the Velociraptor was fierce, smart and fast. One of the most legendary fossils ever found was of this hunter using its powerful foot claw to attack a Protoceratops!

W is for **Wuerhosaurus.**
[woo-er-huh-sawr-us]
Similar to the Stegosaurus, this
dinosaur had two rows of long,
bony plates from its neck all the
way down to its back and tail.
It also ate plants that grew
low to the ground.

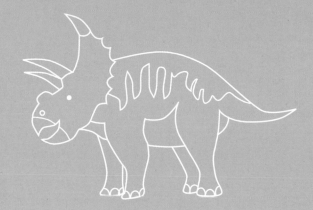

X is for **X**enoceratops.
[zee-no-ser-ah-tops]
With a giant spiked frill and
horns shaped like a spear, 'alien
horned-face' was an earlier cousin
of the Triceratops. It lived around
78 million years ago and was
only discovered in the
year 2012!

Y is for Yunnanosaurus.
[you-nan-oh-sawr-us]
Over 20 specimens have
been found belonging to
Yunnanosaurus, which lived in
Asia around 195 million years ago.
It had spoon-shaped teeth that
rubbed against each other while
it ate as a way of sharpening
themselves!

Z is for Zuniceratops.
[zoo-nee-ser-ah-tops]
Zuniceratops may have been
around 90 million years old, but it
was discovered by an 8-year-old
boy out on a dig with his father! It
just goes to show, you're never too
young to be a paleontologist!

The ever-expanding legendary library

EXPLORE THESE LEGENDARY ALPHABETS & MORE AT WWW.ALPHABETLEGENDS.COM